D1496587

SLEEPING IN THE DEAD GIRL'S ROOM

For Jackie —
Thank you for
coming to the
reading in Plymouth!
♥ Cynthia
12-11-22

Cynthia Bargar

LILY POETRY REVIEW BOOKS

For all the women & girls whose stories were buried with them

Contents

I Churn

II. The Eye

whose place is it to say what happened?

—Rachel Zucker, "A Kind of Catastrophe"

I. Churn

CREATIVE NONFICTION

i.

You, who is the I, are the patient. You & your brother stand in the back of the ambulance. No stretcher, no straps this grey February day. No sirens. No careening down Storrow Drive, or up the Jamaicaway. Your brother pleads, *why are you acting like this? It's not funny.* He walks in the door of the mental hospital with you. Your father is there. Pacing. Does not look at you. You offer him a wallet-sized photo of the swami, your guru. Hope it will calm him down. He says *sign the yellow form. Make it voluntary.* You sign. Despite the shot in the emergency room at the regular hospital, you are still high. They lock you in a ward. You have nothing: no book, no hairbrush, no glasses, no keys. This place is locked up tight. Alarms blink & blare when you try to open the door. Someone always watches. Always sees. This is not sad for you. You are the one who laughs. The only one. An adventure. Like an acid trip. You have no key. Key is not a Metaphor.

ii

The other Cynthia — the She who is
not the I — visits.   Vapor.   The She
is Vapor. Faceless funnel. The She vanishes.

iii

The She who is not the I   haunts & blesses.
The I is driftwood covered with barnacles

As is the She.   The She is organza drenched/illuminated
As is the I.   Who knows this?

Is the haunting a fact? Is the blessing
A truth?

The She appears to be sleeping. The I *is*
Sleeping. The She is gone.   Is this what

Truth is? Always an echo? Not twins.
Because the I   is a body.

The She is Vapor. There are no
Vapor / body twins.   How do you know this?

On the recording your brother
Asks your mother who says

My in-laws had lost their daughter.
We named our daughter after her.

My in-laws. --shh--   --shh--
My in-laws. --shh--   --shh--

iv

Upon release the I who is me, is a
body whose long hair smells like the mental
hospital dumbwaiter. I get a buzz
cut from a friend. My cousin asks *did they buzz
your hair off in that place?* Disbelieves
me when I claim it's a fashion choice.

Lithium makes the body grow fat. I
am round & shorn & will stay like that for years.
Eat cookies all day long, M&M's —
every color. Pair alcohol & lithium
& puke out the car window. Soon will renounce
Jack Daniels   dry vermouth. Later lithium.

Mine is a body in revolt. It asks forgiveness.
Remembers Vapor. Misses Vapor.

v

Cookies. On the recording your mother says
she didn't want you eating cookies all day long.

All day long? Did the I eat them
all day long? You know you did.

Is it too bad your brother didn't
ask your father?   Your father

Would not have answered.
Your father locked   the dead She

away. Would have said
You don't need to know. Stop

asking questions. Too many
questions.   You know your father or do you?

The details & the pictures come
Later.

vi

Maybe one picture. Sylvia
Plath on Winthrop Beach

sunbathing on the rocks
right where you see the She

in the sun on her last day.
You look at the picture of Sylvia

Plath in a book. Your mind
holds the picture of the She.

You know everything
or you think you do

about Sylvia Plath. You know
nothing about the She.

Or maybe it's the other way
around.   A summons.   A haunting.

Listen: mosquitos. Rain &
high tide. They hatch in the marsh
among the cattails—
larvae attach to the roots.
Submerge.   Until mature.

Let's name them Scourge.
Known to enter homes solo
— or coupled at night—
these vampiric bugles devil
our ears. Sneak between
the balusters. Feast 'til blood-drunk.

& then let's not name the She   *--shh--*   *--shh--*
who comes when they call the I.
Nor the I who comes
when they call the She. *--shh--*   *--shh--*

viii

Look: the first Spring robin
Lights upon the rusted monkey sculpture.

Look: crocuses cluster purple
In the sandy ditch by my back door.

If you — the She who is not the I — are
Traveling through give me

A sign: be the fox that slinks across my lawn;
Rustle the vinca on the knoll; tie a ribbon

On the rusted monkey's prehensile tail;
Or frolic with the hatchlings in the birdhouse

Among lint & twigs before you emerge
Covered in nursery dust   to tell me our story.

OTHER CYNTHIA

Rainy day furlough from Glenside
angry you are a mental patient
angry you are compliant
angry you swallow their Haldol
quiver & twitch.

Your mother
drives to Hunan Pagoda swerves
on the VFW Parkway avoids
water-filled craters.

You ask   *--shh--   --shh--*
Did the other Cynthia kill herself?
Yes.
You ask *how.*
Gas. The water heater.

You ask *why.*
We don't know.
Maybe her boyfriend.

Her boyfriend what?
Wasn't Jewish.   *--shh--   --shh--*

You & your mother
round window booth
Hunan Pagoda.
Sip jasmine tea & wait   *--shh--   --shh--*
for egg flower soup
ma po tofu
egg foo yung.
The rain continues   a big sloppy cascade.

CYNTHIA

When they call my name they are calling hers. Calling her.
Inviting her. My namesake. Hers.
One name for both our sakes. My life a name
for her death. We both arrive at the same time. Come when called.

when they call / my name they are calling / hers / calling her /
inviting her / I her / namesake / she / mine
one name / for both / our sakes my life / a name /
for her death we both / arrive at the same time come / when called

HOW YOU GET HERE

you hide in your bed built
on stilts above
your unused desk

your tiny room
your large commune
your small schemes to kill

yourself
at night

night comes & you
imagine
yourself a corpse

wake furious to
be alive
doctor's free samples
pop-out packaging
one blue pill
& you rise

swallow a few more &
you spin
say *I'm cured*

    ***

you go out drinking you
snort some lines you smoke some weed

you cannot stop your body
it sleeps with strangers
this is psycho mind
where you say *excellent*
when they ask "how are you?"

& it's better
it's sparkling   it's jammed

                ***

you walk into Concord Prison
microphone in hand
video camera on your back

say *I am a TV reporter*
here to interview Bud Riley
"sure miss no problem"

the guard brings Bud
you sit on the floor
behind the desk

& from your portapak
you pull the six pack &
the cigarette pack

filled with joints
neatly rolled

your job done
your 20 minutes up
& you are sure Bret

in the high-ceilinged apartment wants
to marry you
wants to take you as his bride

& so you go there
find him in the bathtub
step over the lip

submerge
before you call
Rabbi Wexler

he's known you
since you were a child
ask him to officiate

you call
all your friends
invite them to your wedding

someone decides something's wrong
& right about when
the festivities are to begin

you find yourself here
in the locked ward at
Glenside Hospital

IMPETUOUS TENDENCIES

Patient became excited, preoccupied with sexual thoughts
& denudative.

— author's patient file, Glenside Hospital

The American Journal of Insanity circa 1905 says:
we place satyrs & nymphomaniacs
immediately after the imbecile
& feeble of intellect.

However impetuous be
the tendencies,
the intelligence — if it is normal —
governs & restrains them.

A woman — her lascivious bearing,
provocative movements,
amorous utterances,
— falls to the level of the animal.

Her intellect neither reigns
nor governs.

LOCKED WARD

Winston & Sterling walk me
two flights up to the top floor.
The stench: stale pee.

I ask, *where is the phone?*
"No calls here," Sterling smiles.
"This here's not a hotel, missy."

"You play hearts?" Winston asks.
I fumble my answer, & Sterling
warns, "stay cool missy, stay cool."

HALDOL

Haldol snakes in my bed, tongue depressor
taped to the rusted metal headboard.

…to keep you from swallowing your tongue,
middle of the night, midst of a seizure…

Like Louie, the Boston Terrier with seizures.
My uncle left him with us in Providence
when he took off for Phoenix.

Like Louie, mouth frother, shatterer of flimsy
tongue depressors.   Baffled.   Rigid.
I blink.   I twitch.

YOUR VOLUNTARY COMMITMENT

Does not preclude an escape attempt
— a ride on the dumbwaiter —
after Sterling removes the dinner trays.

Barefoot & laughing you clasp
the contraption — hoist your body
— wriggle until you fit.

You burrow
deep into the metal box
almost locate the switch,

almost lower the door,
almost plunge
the bowels of the building.

Sterling croons:

Funny girl huh? You
be careful.

Laugh too loud,
they take the laugh away.

Enemy combatants you've never
seen — five men, one woman —
drag you down a dark corridor.

An empty room,
a swift shove to the bed,
they tear off your pants.

Pockmarked general jabs
her hypodermic
deep into your thigh.

BREAKFAST AT GLENSIDE

soggy toast / weak
coffee / man
yelling / *time for tv*
/ *time for tv* / devours
mini boxes / rice krispies /
holds one / unopened /
up to his ear / *crackle*

WATER CURE

ambulance unhurried   no sirens howl

nobody's emergency   except her own

        [howl]

first Glenside Hospital admission

26 year old white single female

delivered here
             acutely excited

        [excite]

locked ward
five to a room   no bath   no shower

patient passed
the night   in her clothes

        [pass]

patient moved to single room

the orderly   pinned her
to the bed

forced his way in

        [pin]   [force]

single room   private bathroom

she ran hot water
in the tub
after the orderly left

        [run]

      warm bath a safe and useful remedy
        in this form of disease
      more efficacious if cold
         applied to the head at same time

      < apply >

      temperature of bath
        90 to 100 degrees
      patient may be continued
        an hour or more at a time

      < bathe >

she
whose name
is I

the scalding bath
submerged

        [submerge]

      bath repeated at least every night
        till excitement is removed
      cold shower recommended but like circular swing
        often perceived as punishment

      < repeat >

      < remove >

when head is hot an instinctive desire
    is to apply cold water
many patients seek it themselves
    whenever opportunity presents

< desire >

if efficacy of cold water to head were understood
    in removing paroxysms of excitement
copious bleeding would be less frequent
    and greater numbers would recover from insanity

        [bleed]

< understand >

FROM HER CAME NOT A SOUND

Where is she vanishing?…a girl, almost…
—R.M. Rilke, *Sonnets to Orpheus, I/II*

Midnight. You
alone in the dayroom
reek & linger
dinner odor
over-steamed
vegetables, burnt
hamburger meat.
You watch the night
staff huddle —
four of them play hearts,
fill the nurses' station,
its glass walls aglow.
Night nurse wins, throws
the cards in the air,
hoots.

Your Haldol haze
pierced by the hollers,
you writhe & rise.
Swollen tongue
flutters your mouth
like a frantic baby bird.
Breeze echoes
your name
her name.

You did not lay
a marigold trail for Vapor,
make a welcome altar
or a fire to guide her.
& like you, she eschews
pageantry, vanishes.

BAG OF HEART

She whispers
trust blood & bone
ball & socket.

You motley hobbler,
who does not have
pain?

Cootie catcher? Fortune
teller?
Every baby starts good.

Nature rhymes
without trying.

GHOST LOCKET

Back seat of the sedan,
three-year-old me
leans on my grandmother,
strokes her sealskin coat,

its cool pelts. I look up to
see the locket around her neck.
The girl in the locket
stares back, does not smile.

That's my Cindy, says my grandmother, *she's
in a better place now.* --shh--   --shh--

FIRST FLOOR TOUR: A JUMBLE, A JINX

Living Room

Baby grand, baby me & no more pianist.
Clutching the mahogany leg I rise from the floor.

Leather top coffee table: *Advise and Consent, The Agony and The Ecstasy*
condensed by "Reader's Digest". No readers here.

Dining Room

Pine hutch: dusty hand painted lusterware
teacups. Orange & green guestware. No guests.

KEM plastic playing cards at walnut table's edge: maroon
& green swans play summer solitaire.

Kitchen

Enamel top table: frosted glass cookie jar.
Hostess Sno Balls, Nabisco Mallomars.

White tile counter: one soggy
paper bag stinking of scraps.

AT THE REVERE BEACH WONDERLAND
HIPPODROME CAROUSEL

My cousins tell a story as I mount the medieval
steed, its saddle gilded & jeweled — flower
garland, sapphire & saffron, carved in deep relief.

> *at the flying horse factory in India*
> *snakes often dart into a horse's mouth*
> *& give birth to snake babies*
> *who ship to America inside the horses*
>
> *& when a little girl like you*
> *rides a flying horse*
> *a snake might dart out*
> *& wrap itself around her neck*

Eyes shut, legs wedged, I gallop up to the rafters,
crash down, helpless to quell the wooden beast,
the calliope's whirr & whine.

DDT

We all breathe salt air, sunbathe
on a tombolo that is our beach,
green railings to Cottage Hill. Trudge
a low-tide sandspit out to five
breakers we call the Five Sisters.
Later, walk home.

At dusk the uprising. Mosquitoes
depart the marshes for the backyards,
their wrathful wing-drone
synchronized to our garden-watering.
Desperate, in search of blood, females
nourish their eggs, force us inside.

In the morning planes fly low,
spray poison. Our open windows.

PRESUMABLY

The Commonwealth of Massachusetts
DEPARTMENT OF PUBLIC HEALTH
REGISTRY OF VITAL RECORDS AND STATISTICS   R 3⁷1074

SUFFOLK
(County)
WINTHROP
(City or Town)
No. 254 Main St.,

The Commonwealth of Massachusetts
OFFICE OF THE SECRETARY
DIVISION OF VITAL STATISTICS
MEDICAL EXAMINER'S
CERTIFICATE OF DEATH

WINTHROP
(City or town making return)
Registered No. 167
(If death occurred in a hospital or institution,
St. give its NAME instead of street and number)

FULL NAME   CYNTHIA BARGAR
(If deceased is a married, widowed or divorced woman, give also maiden name.)

Physician — Important
{ Was deceased a
U. S. War Veteran,
if so specify WAR}

(a) Residence. No. 254 Main   St.
(Usual place of abode)   (If nonresident, give city or town and State)

Length of stays in hospital or institution   —   years   months   days.   In this community   yrs.   mos.   days.
(before death)   (Specify whether)

PERSONAL AND STATISTICAL PARTICULARS

4 COLOR OR RACE	5 SINGLE (write the word) MARRIED WIDOWED or DIVORCED
SEX Female	White Single

If married, widowed, or divorced
HUSBAND of
(a) WIFE of   (Give maiden name of wife in full)
(Husband's name in full)

Age of husband or wife if alive   years

IF STILLBORN, enter that fact here.

AGE 18 Years 4 Months 8 Days   If less than 1 day Hours Minutes

Usual
Occupation   Student
Industry
or Business   B. U.
Social Security No.
BIRTHPLACE (City,   Boston
State or country)   Mass.   30

MEDICAL CERTIFICATE OF DEATH

18 DATE OF DEATH   August   24   1947
(Month)   (Day)   (Year)

19 I HEREBY CERTIFY that I have investigated the death
of the person above-named and that the CAUSE AND MANNER thereof
are as follows: (If an injury was involved, state fully.)

Gas Poisoning 16⅓hr

Presumably Suicidal

20. Accident, suicide, or homicide (specify)
Date of occurrence August 24   19

Where did
Injury occur?   Winthrop
(City or town and State)
Did injury occur in or about home, on farm, in industrial place, or in
public place?   Home
(Specify type of place)

Manner of
Injury   Found dead in a gas
Nature of
Injury   filled room at her home.
While at work?   —   Was there an autopsy?   No

21 Was disease or injury in any way related to occupation of deceased?   —
If so, specify
(Signed)   Wm. J. Brickley   M. D.
(Address)   Boston   Date 8/25 19 47

22 Ahavas Achim Anshe Sfaard, Lynn
Place of Burial, Cremation or Removal.   (City or Town)
DATE OF BURIAL   August 26, 19 47

23 NAME OF
FUNERAL DIRECTOR   Benj. F. Solomon
ADDRESS   420 Harvard St., Brookline
Received and filed   August 29 19 47

A TRUE COPY ATTEST: (Registrar)

The She who died by gas
 - a suicide? An accident?

Family & medical examiner at odds.
Autopsy or not?

They do concur it occurred
at home   254 Main.

The She who is I & did not die
 lived there. Slept in the dead girl's room.

Dean DiMartino
Acting Registrar of Vital Records and Statistics

I, the above signed, hereby certify that I am the Registrar of Vital Records and Statistics;
that as such I have custody of the records of birth, marriage, and death required by law to
be kept in my office; and I do hereby certify that the above is a true copy from said records.
IT IS ILLEGAL TO ALTER OR REPRODUCE THIS DOCUMENT IN ANY MANNER

CELLAR

He entered through the cellar door, kicked aside dirty tea towels decorated with smiling housewives & strawberries, dishrags marred by chocolate & gravy, wine-stained tablecloths embroidered in my grandmother's clumsy cross-stitch, shades of jade & violet. Ever since that August night, my grandmother avoided the cellar. When she flung the washing down her ersatz laundry chute, some pieces draped the railings, some sprinkled the steps, others pooled at the bottom. They waited for my grandfather to gather them in his arms & bring them into the utility room. The room where *--shh--   --shh--*. Their dead girl. Their Cindy.

FRIDAY NIGHT AT 254 MAIN

My grandmother slides a Mallomar through
the balusters. Music from Bonanza &

my grandfather's cigar smoke
drift up from the cellar

where he types the bills
for the family rag business.

His black Underwood & tube radio
grace the round table, its leather top scratched.

His cigar will shrink in the ashtray,
as he pecks the typewriter keys. His chair

close to the spot where, five years before,
he found her.

A FULL DAY AT THE BEACH

Sun scorching your shoulders,
you lingered past dusk,
long after the others
danced the sand for last clam
bubbles, filled their pails
& paraded home for supper.

You stayed, early evening — the heat,
the lowest tide, the stench.

When darkness engulfed you rolled up
your blanket & walked home.

254 MAIN

My mother, expecting to bleed,
fastened each end of the gauzy pad
to the sanitary belt
slung snug below her waist.

Forsaking her white bathing suit
for navy blue Bermuda shorts &
a light blue sleeveless blouse,
she tied the laces on her clean white Keds.

You could say I was there,
heard the echo, her body in motion.

***

Was this how it went? My mother reached
the seawall, Winthrop Beach,
wondered whether breakfast — a poached egg on
toast — or the heat had rendered her queasy?

Did my father appear? Cozy up?
Run barefoot over the rocks & dive in?

Did he swim from the Green Bars
to Water Tower Hill before the walk home
for garden tomatoes dressed in sour cream,
buttered black bread on the side?
You could say I was there.

***

I must have heard her gasp
on the telephone —
break
the news to my father.

The silent one-mile ride to 254 Main,
the rush into the house,
Cindy's body on the gurney,
before the men covered her.

You could say I was there.

***

Every day upstairs
bathroom my mother
— vomiting —
not bleeding.

23 years old, she hid
her changing body
out of respect
for sorrow. The family.

Did she cling to my father at night,
tremble in his narrow
childhood bed, unable
to close her eyes?

Once he was asleep did she rise,
wander through a narrow doorway
& in the morning did he find us
sleeping in a dead girl's room?

SLEEPING IN THE DEAD GIRL'S ROOM

sharp piano   no no

worship   the shrill harmony

I   crib

I baby   pinpoint blue

voice   hi lo

distant   tanager

deeper   treble

moans & creases

beneath the hill

pray   a night flower

                        a moon warbler

                        rhubarb

bruised

patina

TIDAL

cloud-covered
ill-omened   gunmetal
August night

driftwood   debris

falling towards
water

beached seal baitfish
stranded silver peanut bunker

her hand   squeezing

wet sand

drip castle
encrustation   pebbles
glass

the end
piling at the end

what is tidal

MY AUNT TALKS TO SYLVIA PLATH

What the sluttish, rutted sea could do.
— Sylvia Plath, "Point Shirley"

Your sluttish, rutted sea churned up
trouble for our families. Some
call Winthrop-by-the-Sea
a fitting childhood home for you,
your words embalmed with moist & misty
beach breaths razored like the clams
we loved to dig. I left behind little proof of
that place fitting or not fitting.

Your grandmother's Point Shirley
geranium bed with a hurricane-pounded
shark startled six-year-old you, while
a mile away & three years older,
I watched tall pines sway, dip,
crack in my front yard,
hostas airborne, their leaves
like propellers on the planes
whose lights we both craved,
landing nightly at Logan.

After the storm, did I push you
on the swing at Ingleside Park?
Did our mothers, Dorothy & Aurelia,
nod, never speak, each
already afraid? When the bell rang
I believe it was you who chased me
up the hill to the Willis School.

I chose to die
during an August heat wave.
You may have heard it was gas.

VIGIL   [Immediately After]

& they huddle clutching
        memories in a teacup   orange rim chipped

TO CINDY, IS THIS HOW I WILL RESURRECT YOU?

A sculpture
in a portico,
a lily in my garden?
I don't know
what would be fitting.
Cindy May Bargar
of Winthrop. My
father's one sister.
Cindy of the night
beach. Cindy air,
Cindy vapor. You escaped,
left me the name.

II. The Eye

MY GRANDMOTHER AT THE CLAM STAND

She tips a clam roll sideways
in its cardboard jacket.
Her fingers long
like mine. Chipped nail
polish, wild rose.
How she smothers the clams,
creamy tartar sauce
laced with piccalilli,
& how her bites,
though careful,
tumble crumbs to gravel.

WRAPPED IN RED

Relapses are most frequent in autumn in those whose veins are most full.
— American Journal of Insanity

The floor's strewn with rolling balls of red.
I pick one up. Put it down, brew a cup of tea.
Fortified, I cast on &
knit.

Fall comes. Undone.
Wool stitches don't
conceal the bulge of my veins.

I bind myself
in the red sweater-coat,
the too-long belt
around my middle again
& again, then
trek through
neighborhoods
oblivious.

AFTER *INFINITELY POLAR BEAR* AT THE COOLIDGE CORNER CINEMA

[In the ladies' room line I am moody.]

Did you like Polar Bear?

            It was good, I mumble.

You must see *Love & Mercy.* That's the other mental health movie.
As a former mental health worker I love the genre.

            As a former mental patient I do too.

[Her turn for a toilet.]

[Another mental health moth is drawn to my flame]:

I'm bipolar just like the father. Fine until 40.

            I was locked up at 26. They called it manic depression.

What are you on? Lithium like him? I took it for two days. Terrible.

            I took it for six years. Burning.

You know we are miracles   don't you? Don't you?

        Are we? Are we?

THREE QUALMS

1.
Before I traveled through a body into a body, who was I?
        — Kazim Ali, "The Plaint of Marah, Woman of Sodom"

Water exhausted, unable to breathe. Aching for
      a heart to listen — to see
the surface.   To hover over the strange & tiny sea.
      Uncloaked. Bruised: for thrift,
limbs, organza.

2.
She saw herself bereft
of body.
        — Susan Howe, *The Nonconformist's Memorial*

In the moment of falling
I blame cobblestones;
      pale baby in a padded helmet,
         squirming in the stroller, lips parched and cracked;
    a tiny bird   under the left front wheel —
       a few bloody feathers in the gutter.

3.
I don't remember anything.
You don't either.
        — Michael Burkard, "Anti-Memoir (Moon Death)"

Girl in a locket, a trace, a stone.
I polish the stone   carry it in my pocket
        wear it around my neck.
When I swap it for a glass globe
      two dewy irises glisten on my windshield
        tucked under the wipers —
          buds about to burst.

SNAKE SLUT

you say you
can never
look

but you always
do

take that painted
u-haul
slowed to slinking
on 8th avenue

       eleven red-sided
       garter snakes

       three
       red tongues
       impossibly
       long

       eight
       mouths
       clamped shut

       the way
       they form
       a phalanx
       look
       like plants
       sprouting

you
adrenalize
pacify
cajole

say
crazy to be
afraid of a snake-
painted
u-haul
in Manhattan
traffic

        eleven
        fragments
        flirt you
        beckon

you
cannot
          resist

SOMETIMES THE NATURE OF THINGS

My mother's leg [veins]. Ropey lumpy blue knots. A surgeon

slits her groin, hooks the bulging culprits, pulls. Everything

is snake: her veins, surf's imprint on sand, mountain ridge above the bay, ether-

net cable under the desk, [umbilical cord] around unbirthed baby's neck.

AT THE SNAKE & SPIDER PHOBIA STUDY

electrodermal
response
sensors filigree
our fingers
like jewelry
from an ancient future

we submit

king-sized
slides —
mushrooms
spiders flowers
snakes
slugs
& a crocodile —

electrotactile
stimulators
bewilder
our
bodies

alarm
our   amygdalae

PILGRIM'S DREAM

Fort Point Channel mute swans
lower their necks to lunch
beneath the sudsy brine.
I leave them, cross A Street,
find my car, take Haul Road & follow
a maze of red & yellow sky-puncturing
cranes, until Logan Airport is in plain view,
Winthrop-by-the-Sea tucked behind.

& I drive the Ted Williams tunnel,
zip through East Boston
& once arrived in Winthrop,
slow to glimpse the old house,
254 Main. Front yard
shorn of its tall pines,
chartreuse café curtains
where once hung
brocade drapes ceiling to floor,
mauve roses on a grey field.

I park seaside,
hike Shore Drive
up the Highlands
to the Cliff House,
grand hotel turned
nursing home
in time for my grandfather
to be moved in.

Then to 21 James Avenue, dead-end,
where the blond
German neighbor boy
chased me with his pet snake,
locked me in his garage & when
he let me out, garden hose
draped over his shoulder,
shot me with jets of cold water.

YOU RETURN TO YOUR FORT POINT APARTMENT

Fight the lock that always sticks,
open the door & find your grandfather
lounging on the sofa.
Hazy blue cigar smoke
billows. He says,
I'm here with my Cindy.

NINE DAYS BEFORE YOUR DEATH

i.

This photo. Unposed.
Black & white. Smile
lingers seductive, fresh.
No disquiet in your eyes.

ii.

Your hair kerchiefed,
a few curls undone,
reminders —
this is summer.

iii.

Summer captures
the swell of your breasts;
the rumpled ruffle under
your sunlit clavicle.

iv.

You grip a vanilla cone. One scoop.
It drips, speckles your fingers.

v.

Smitten with the one behind the camera.

vi.

Beautiful, not because we are
blood.   No. Not that desire
to imbue one's dead
kin with beauty.

vii.

Everlasting girlgrace. So
unlike our women: frowsy
uterine ancestors.
Their loose housedresses.

viii.

A tall tree behind you
— looms.

ix.

Composed,
you walk toward me
almost out of frame.

MY TWO CENTURIES

Lady sits on her stool, paws
pictures of human eyes.
Shared name buried in a hatbox.

Says to create the earth,
visit that sinking house.
Be a suspect.

***

Dear life in my pocket, cheap life
tight underground, my fingers
tug at buttons. They ask me
to uncover the imprint: skin on fire,
the hair, the bones,
stones etched by lightning.

MIDRASH ON NAMING

name a child for a deceased loved one
        & that soul will shine on through the child

unless the loved one suffered
an unnatural death   *--shh--*   *--shh--*

drug overdose
homicide
suicide

misfortune   (dormant until stirred)
will find the child

suicide *(--shh--*   *--shh--)*   *don't name it*

A FICTION

you don't die
　　　　let's say my name is Jody

　　　when your parents learn
　　　　　　you　　　are pregnant

　　　they won't allow you
　　　　　　to live　　　　at 254 main

　　　your brother　　　　who will become my father
　　　　　　invites you to move in

　　　with him　　　& his wife
　　　　　　you give birth to your son

　　　let's call him Simon
　　　one month later　　　my mother has me

　　　Simon & I
　　　　　　cousin twins

let's say my name is Joanne

you anger your parents
try   to be good

Latin club president
        vestal virgin

how could you
                who are you

you have a boyfriend let's
call him Duncan

his parents
    fold you in

he drives you
        to your college classes

picks you up
        after working at the marina

Duncan too
        tries to be good

you move from 254 main
            live with Duncan & his parents

you are Cynthia
I am Joanne   your baby niece

so alive are you
as you push my stroller up & down the Crest

iii

   let's say my name is Josephine

you marry your boyfriend
let's call him Mike

a civil ceremony   judge's chambers
no family in attendance

— you are dead to them mirrors
draped with black cloth

your brown baby a boy my cousin
let's call him Jacob

he like you
a whisper a frown

your brother & his wife
pregnant with me

move in with your parents
they are bereft

— you are dead to them
you are not dead

Notes:

Water Cure

Author's Intake Record, Glenside Hospital

"Medical Treatment of Insanity," *American Journal of Insanity*, Volume VII, July, 1850

Gas Kills Girl in Winthrop

"Gas Kills Girl in Winthrop," *The Lowell Sun*, August 25, 1947, p. 11

Presumably

Cynthia Bargar, death certificate, 24 Aug. 1947

Wrapped in Red

"The Frequency of Relapse in Insanity," *American Journal of Insanity*, Vol XIX, No. 1, July 1862

Midrash on Naming

"A Jewish Rose by Any Other Name: Thoughts on the Regulation of Jewish Women's Personal Names," Omi (Naomi) Morgenstern Leissner, *Women in Judaism: A Multidisciplinary Journal*, Volume 14 Number 1, 2017

"The Do's and Don'ts of Jewish Baby Naming," Eric Schucht, *Jewish Exponent*, 23 Oct. 2019

"Naming a Son for a Brother Who Died Young," Linda K. Wertheimer, Motherlode, *The New York Times*, 22 July 2012

Acknowledgements

My gratitude to the following publications in which these poems or earlier versions first appeared (sometimes with different titles):

LUMINA Literary Journal: "My Two Centuries"

Apeiron Review: "Three Qualms" and "After Seeing *Infinitely Polar Bear* at the Coolidge Corner Cinema"

Driftwood Press: "Sleeping in the Dead Girl's Room" and "Other Cynthia"

Stoneboat Literary Journal and *Stoneboat 10th Anniversary Retrospective*: "A Fiction"

The Loch Raven Review: "Locked Ward" and "How You Get Here"

Poems2go: "Wrapped in Red"

The Comstock Review: "254 Main"

Book of Matches: "At the Revere Beach Wonderland Hippodrome Carousel"

Rogue Agent: "Impetuous Tendencies" and "Haldol"

Twelve Mile Review: "Creative Nonfiction"

All my thanks to Joe Bargar, Erica Bronstein, Eileen Cleary, Wendy Drexler, Vivian Eyre, Fine Arts Work Center, Kelle Groom, Nadia Herman Colburn, Marianne Hirsch, Barbara Iannoli, Kevin McLellan, Martha McCollough, Napa Valley Writers Conference, KPrevallet, and Brian Turner.

My love and gratitude to Nick Thorkelson, my first reader and keeper of my flame, and to Ruby T, for the gorgeous cover image and for always knowing when a poem of mine is not fully cooked.

About the Author

Author photo by Erica Bronstein

Cynthia Bargar's poems have appeared in *Rogue Agent,*
Book of Matches, LUMINA Literary Journal, Comstock Review,
Driftwood Press, Stoneboat Literary Journal, and other journals.
Sleeping in the Dead Girl's Room is her debut collection. Her
prose poem, "Beach at St. Mary's," is included in the new book
of images and text, *Our Provincetown: Intimate Portraits* by
Barbara E. Cohen (Provincetown Arts Press, 2021). Cynthia
is associate poetry editor at *Pangyrus LitMag.* She lives in
Provincetown, Massachusetts with cartoonist Nick Thorkelson.

CPSIA information can be obtained
at www.ICGtesting.com
Printed in the USA
JSHW021540310522
26470JS00007B/177